A TIME TO KEEP

CHERIE FLEISCHMAN GOREN

A MEMOIR OF GROWING UP IN MEMEL, LITHUANIA,
AND COMING TO AMERICA
IN 1939

A TIME TO KEEP, AND A TIME TO LOSE;
A TIME TO KEEP, AND A TIME TO CAST AWAY
ECCLESIASTES   3:6

ISBN: 9781090987853

Imprint: Independently published

Edited by Ellen Sue Spicer-Jacobson (2nd edition)
ellensuespicerjacobson@gmail.com

Designed by Krista Nelson
knelsonauthor@gmail.com

TABLE OF CONTENTS

Moses Golden Pajuris, Russia-Naturalized British in Dublin ——

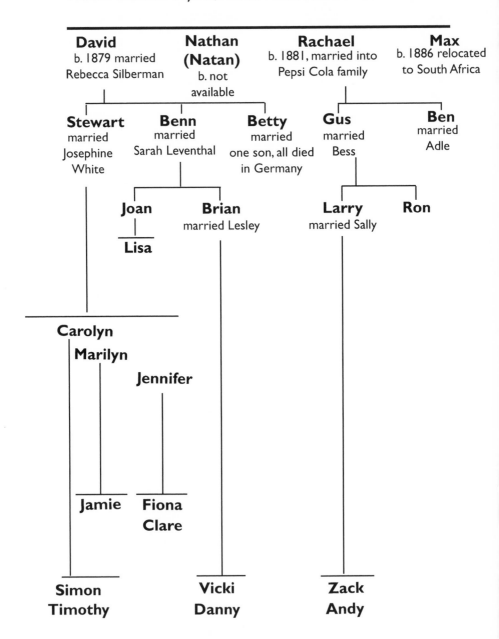

David
b. 1879 married
Rebecca Silberman

**Nathan
(Natan)**
b. not
available

Rachael
b. 1881, married into
Pepsi Cola family

Max
b. 1886 relocated
to South Africa

Stewart
married
Josephine
White

Benn
married
Sarah Leventhal

Betty
married
one son, all died
in Germany

Gus
married
Bess

Ben
married
Adle

Joan

Brian
married Lesley

Larry
married Sally

Ron

Lisa

Carolyn

Marilyn

Jennifer

Jamie

Fiona

Clare

Simon
Timothy

Vicki
Danny

Zack
Andy

Kende Golden East Prussia, city unknown

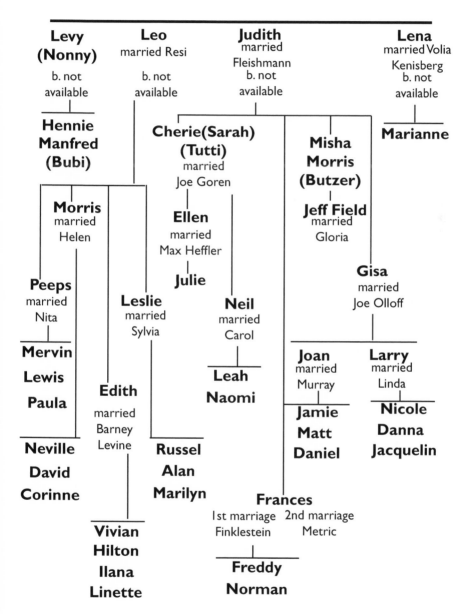

Caption text within tree:

Levy (Nonny)
b. not available
— **Hennie Manfred (Bubi)**

Leo married Resi
b. not available

Judith married Fleishmann
b. not available

Lena married Volia Kenisberg
b. not available
— **Marianne**

Cherie(Sarah) (Tutti) married Joe Goren
— **Ellen** married Max Heffler
— **Julie**

Misha Morris (Butzer)
— **Jeff Field** married Gloria

Morris married Helen

Peeps married Nita
— **Mervin Lewis Paula** — **Neville David Corinne**

Leslie married Sylvia
— **Edith** married Barney Levine
— **Vivian Hilton Ilana Linette**

Neil married Carol
— **Leah Naomi**

Gisa married Joe Olloff

Joan married Murray
— **Jamie Matt Daniel**

Larry married Linda
— **Nicole Danna Jacquelin**

Russel Alan Marilyn

Frances
1st marriage Finklestein   2nd marriage Metric
— **Freddy Norman**

Family Tree was created by family in South Africa.

INTRODUCTION

I WAS MADE aware of my daughter Ellen's misconception about my childhood when I took her to see the play, "Fiddler on the Roof," when she was in college. She remarked, "Oh, Mother, now I know where you came from." I sat down and wrote this memoir in one afternoon to set the facts straight. I also wrote this book for my current family and future heirs so they would understand that my childhood in Lithuania was a beautiful time to keep.

MEMEL:

G RAMMY CHERIE'S STORY

GROWING UP IN MEMEL IN THE 1930s,
in retrospect, brings back the stories of Hans
Christian Andersen's "Beautiful Port by the Sea." And so it
was, only the ending was so different — unspeakable.
Memelland (Memel's name before WWI when part of
Germany) represented the height of German-Jewish culture.
It was easy to think of ourselves as princesses. We were four
children: Fanny, Sarah (I was called "Tutti"), Gisela (called
"Gisa"), and Misha (called "Butzer"). Our father, Leo Fleischmann,⁺ was a distributor of textiles for Lithuania. He spent
the mornings at his store and the afternoons at the bridge club
or a café. He spent the summers in Czechoslovakia, either
Karlsbad or Marienbad, for the *kuhr** (the German word for
health cure). We were transported to a place called Schwartzort, a village resort on the peninsula from Memel to the Baltic
Sea. It was a short boat ride across the bay to our summer
home, the Villa Lieselotte.

⁺*Changed to Fleischman in America*
**Italicized words with translation in parentheses are almost all Yiddish, with a*
few in German. I learned some Yiddish in America.

My mother, the former Judith Golden, was very busy. She supervised a cook and a *Fräulein*, an unmarried nursemaid and housemaid combined. A laundress came in once a week and a seamstress twice a year. We also had a car, a black luxury sedan, and of course, a chauffeur to go with it. We rarely rode in it. We could run through the city in no time at all. It seemed my mother was always running from the fish market with a large shopping net. Being a seaport, the fish market was large and exciting. Long, wooden tables lined the wharf; live fish jumped on the planks. No respectable housewife would buy a dead fish.

Many tradespeople came to our door: the butter-and-egg woman, the vegetable farmer, etc. I think she went to the *shochet* (the kosher butcher) with her big net for the chicken and other meat. She picked a live chicken. We watched with queasy fascination as the *shochet* slaughtered it according to Jewish law. He then handed it to the "chicken flicker," covered with feathers, who plucked the chicken by hand with feathers flying in all directions. I always managed to get a nice large feather for my collection.

Let's start with my grandfather, Moses Golden. He was an Irish Jew. He moved from Ireland to Lithuania to give his sons a good Jewish education, Lithuania being the seat of Jewish culture. Jews had lived in Lithuania since the middle of the 18th century. Moses and Kende had eight children: Rachel, David, Max, Leo, Judith (my mother), Nacham (called "Nonny"), Lena, and Nathan ("Natan").

Moses established the Schwartzen Adler Hotel. He was a tall, strong Irishman, who, nevertheless, got pneumonia and died young. My mother's older brother, David, had another business that was well-established. Max went to South Africa. Rachel was married to Robert Domont and moved to America, while Leo had a thriving shoe store. So, my mother Judith, a beautiful girl in her twenties with many suitors, assumed the management of the hotel.

Leo Fleischmann, one of the guests from Riga, Latvia, was the youngest of his four siblings. He had a brother, Robert. Nothing is known of him. He had three sisters: Mary, Charlotte, and Johanna. His mother, Ella Fleischmann Birkholtz, a handsome, brilliant woman, was a scribe, and Leo was the apple of her eye. He was very handsome, spoke six languages, had a photographic memory, and above all, was a charmer. The ladies adored him.

He fled to Lithuania from Riga to avoid conscription into the Russian Army. Leo knocked on the door of the Schwartzen Adler in the middle of the night. Judith admitted him. There was no room at the inn, being filled to capacity with all the escapees from the war as well as tradespeople. However, she took one look at this handsome stranger and made him a bed in the dining room on the table, or so the story goes. They fell in love instantly.

She reluctantly gave up all her suitors. They married as quickly as they could. Judith was 30 years old, and Leo was 23. Her mother cried since Judith was "so young." (This secret was kept so well that Leo never knew of the age difference. We found out only when Mama applied for Social Security after Leo had died.) Leo had gone into business with Judith's financial assistance and he soon became successful. Lithuania had textile mills and Leo became a textile distributor. He also imported textiles from England and lace from Belgium. The limousine they owned was used mostly by his salesmen to travel the provinces. Leo and Judith moved into a spacious apartment in a fashionable part of town and raised their family of three girls and a boy: Fanny, me (Sarah/"Tutti"), Gisa, and Misha ("Butzer").

1900 - Golden Family Photo with my mother, Judith Golden (standing center) with her mother Kende, father Moses, and four of her seven siblings.

1907- My mother, Judith Golden

1910 - My grandfather, Moses Golden (seated)
with my Uncle Leo (standing)

Early 1900s - My mother, Judith Golden,
with her brother Leo Golden

1916 - David Golden (my mother Judith's oldest brother)
with wife Rebecca

1917- Judith Golden (my mother)

The Schwartzen Adler ceased to exist as a hotel and was converted into apartments. Nonny occupied one apartment and continued to operate the tavern. David lived in another with his wife, Rebecca; two sons, Beno and Siegfried; and a daughter, Betty. Another apartment housed Leo, his wife Resi, and four children: Morris, Sigmund (called "Peeps"), Edith, and Lacka. Their age range was the same as ours. Our parents must have planned our coexistence. The last apartment belonged to my widowed grandmother, Kende, who lived there with her youngest son, my Uncle Nathan, always called Natan.

The Schwartzen Adler had a large L-shaped courtyard. The apartments lined the L. Across one side, away from the rooms, there was a horse stable. My grandmother also had a cow and goats. My mother often spoke of the goats' milk and cheese, which they had been raised on, and she attributed her good health and longevity to them. She lived to 104.

The front of the hotel was on Friedrich Strasse. On the corner was The Tavern. In the front diagonal was a large marketplace, the Friedrichmark, where the farmers and tradespeople conducted their business and frequented the tavern. The surrounding area consisted of little, narrow streets with small, congested houses. It was called Old Town; mostly orthodox Jews from Poland, Russia, and Eastern Europe lived there. The rest of the town started at the canal, which flowed from the bay into the Baltic Sea. The canal separated the old town from the newer city of tree-lined, broad streets, buildings with ornate façades containing apartments, stores, and cafés. German Jews had settled there and flourished in a climate of acceptance and tolerance. They were prosperous. They owned banks, and lumber and textile mills. They were professionals: doctors, lawyers, and merchants.

Late 1800s - Leo Fleischmann (my father)
with my grandmother Ella Fleischmann - late 1800s

(The double "n" at the end of the name was dropped when our family
migrated to America and our name became Fleischman.)

Family photo of family in the Courtyard
of the Schwartzen Adler Hotel that
my mother owned and managed.

Left to Right (front):
Aunt Rachel, my grandmother Kende, Nathan (Natan)

Back row:
My cousin Siegfriend, my uncle David's son.

We lived in a large apartment on Liebauer Strasse. The building had a large bay window, so we had full view of the street in both directions. We lived on the second floor. A wide staircase led to our apartment. The entrance had a wide glass door, and to the right were 22 built-in closets that ran the length of the long hall that led to the kitchen. My brother Butzer loved to ride his tricycle in that hall. Opposite the closets were bedrooms followed by small rooms for the help, and the bathroom, which held a hot water heater. The living room was to the left of the front door, at the front of the apartment. The bay window had a step that created a small stage. Fanny considered herself an actress. I was a dancer and Gisa, the singer. Butzer would heckle us while sitting on top of the armoire, out of sight, behind a large clock. My parents' friends had to suffer through many of our performances. My father thought we were perfect children and could do no wrong.

A large courtyard was in the rear of the building. The laundry was housed in a corner of the yard. A laundress came in once a week and, with the help of the cook and *Fräulein*, they would heat water in huge tubs, wash the clothes, and hang the sheets on rods to dry. They pressed them by placing them on large, wooden rollers and turning a large wheel, rolling them through. I guess this was a hand press. Clothing that could not be washed, like wool dresses and suits, were dipped in kerosene and hung out to dry until the fumes evaporated.

We liked playing in the courtyard with the janitor's children and others in the building. During the week of *Pesach* (Passover) all the children disappeared. I once knocked on the janitor's door to ask if his children could come out. I was told that Jews kill little children for their blood ritual on *Pesach*. This form of anti-Semitism was prevalent in Europe, going back to the Crusades. It was especially common with Lithuanian peasants, who were also very superstitious. When I told Papa, he forbade us to go near what he called "those ignorant, superstitious peasants."

In the canal were many boats, small ships, and a large ferry. The ferry crossed the Kurishe Nehrung Bay between Memel and Königsberg on the Baltic Sea. A resort called Sandkrug was a fifteen-minute ride across the bay. The narrow peninsula ran along the bay, separating the bay from the sea. At one end was the port of Memel, Lithuania, which opened to the Baltic Sea, and at the other end was Germany.

Restaurants, lemonade and ice cream stands lined the landing pier, where the ferry docked. As one walked away from the pier, the road went through a magnificent pine forest. Past the pier were cafés with very chic people and music, mostly violins. There were also tennis courts, where people watched men in white flannel slacks play a game. Croquet was also very fashionable. A house up on the hill featured a casino. As the road continued, the forest became thicker and the air more pungent with pine. Gradually, a large, very sandy hill came into view and, as we reached the peak, we saw the Baltic Sea. A panorama of dunes, covered with some sea grass and the sparkling sea, was breathtakingly beautiful. There were people bathing and gathering *bernstein* (the semi-precious stone, amber). In front of the dunes were small cabanas that one could rent by the day for changing into swimwear.

In the summer before we moved to our summer villa in Schwarzort, my cousins and I would often take the ferry and go to the beach. We were allowed to go without supervision, since it was not considered dangerous. The woods were filled with wild blueberries, strawberries, huckleberries, raspberries and mushrooms. We would fill our small buckets to take home, or just lie under a bush and stuff ourselves.

In the winter it was cold. The windows were frosted over. I would scratch a hole to see through. Ice castles, flowers and fairies were visible on the window panes — with a little imagination — and through the small hole we could see chimney sweepers dressed in black with high hats carrying long ladders. Sometimes I could spot a stork in his nest on a roof. I wore long, wool stockings held up by garter belts. Many days we went ice skating. Even with my wool stockings I got frostbitten. My mother put goose fat on it. I guess it worked, since I still have my legs.

The winter days were short and dark came very early, but in the summer, there was light until 11 p.m. Sometimes for a special treat my father — We called him Papa — would hire a large horse-drawn sleigh. The sleigh had thick blankets inside. My parents and the small children would be tucked in. My boy cousins and I would tie our small sleds to the back of the large sleigh with bells. We rode through the beautiful forest and stopped at a café for hot chocolate and pastries. We had to be very careful not to fall off, since we were going pretty fast. I can't believe my parents let us do this!

Once Papa agreed to go ice skating with me, and the whole town turned out to watch. I was not a very good skater; my ankles always turned in. I tripped him. He fell and cracked his rib on my skate. So much for winter sports.

1927 Memel - L. to R.
My older sister Fanny, Mama and me (Cherie /"Tutti")

1929 Memel - L. to R.
Older sister Fanny, me (Cherie /"Tutti")
and younger sister Gisa. Baby brother
Misha ("Butzer") was born in 1931

1934 Memel - Group photo of members of Betar,
A Zionist organization. I am in the front row;
Fanny is in the back row.

1935 - Papa
My father, Leo Fleischmann

MY SCHOOL YEARS

WHEN I WAS SIX, my mother tried to register me for school. I was weighed in wearing my gray Persian lamb coat and boots and was rejected since I only weighed 18 kilos (approximately 40 pounds). Mother immediately enrolled me in a gymnastic class to build me up. A group of us puny kids had to play with a large medicine ball. I hated it and ducked when the ball came my way. I didn't last there very long. The instructor found me uncooperative.

Then, I joined the Maccabees (a Jewish gymnastics club). My uncle, Nathan Golden, was very involved with this organization and promised to keep an eye on me. I liked the gymnastics and was soon swinging from the bars. We wore blue shorts and white tops. We were told to appear for a group photo. I forgot and wore a black leotard and really stood out in the picture. Ping-Pong was really my favorite game. I played until I left Memel in 1938. When I was twelve, I became junior Ping-Pong champion (of what I am not sure). I played against all the boys. Mother had the dining room table opened for me and my friends, all boys, and we played every day.

1935 - My little brother Misha ("Butzer") and me
on the pier in Schwartzort

1936 - Mama (far left), friend, Papa, friend (far right)
in Karlsbad, Czeckoslovakia, for the *kuhr*
(at a healthspa) "The ladies adored him!"

Early to mid - 1930s:
A guest house in Schwarzort (top)
and the path through the forest to the sea (bottom)

Finally, I was enrolled in school. They had to take me — it was the law. My sister Fanny and I went to a German school. In elementary school we were taught embroidery and knitting. Once I entered the Lyceum, I spent a lot of time dissecting sentences. We also spent much time on geography, studying what once was Germany, but was now Lithuania.

After school I had to go to an apartment where two old, smelly ladies, genteel and fallen on hard times, helped children of all ages with their homework. I guess German schools were hard. We memorized Goethe and Schiller. We sang songs by Heinrich Heine. At home I had to take piano lessons. I am tone deaf and have punctured eardrums. I played the same piece at my recital for two years before I was allowed to quit. Papa always sent me flowers.

Memel belonged to Germany before World War I and had been in East Prussia. It was given to Lithuania after they carved up Germany at Versailles. The population was divided, mostly German, under Lithuanian rule. A great portion of Jews identified with the Germans and their culture. There were also the *Ostjuden* (the Eastern European Jews). Lithuania encouraged them to settle in Memel, to help establish a more Eastern European climate. The *Ostjuden* children were not in the German schools and we did not mix. I think the Jews invented snobbery.

The German Jews in Lithuania were very assimilated, but they clung to their Orthodox ways. They were educated at the universities and moved with ease in the mainstream of European politics, arts, and commerce. They were fluent in several languages and dressed in the latest fashions. They considered themselves elitist German Jews and found the eastern European Jews to be an embarrassment.

These Eastern Jews from Poland and Russia, who were barred from secular education and many professions in their homelands, clung to their *shtetl* (village) ways. Most went to the famous Yeshiva in Vilna, Lithuania, and continued to wear the traditional garb of long black coats and hats, fringed undergarments, and *peyos* (sidelocks or curls). These *Ostjuden* spoke Yiddish at home and among one another. They observed Jewish law to the letter and kept to themselves. After all, Lithuania was considered the seat of Jewish culture with the Yeshiva in Vilna as its base. Their Yiddish dialect was different. They used the letter U instead of I. They said "tunkle" while Jews in Galizia said "*tinkle*" (dark). They looked down on the Galitzianer Jews from southern Russia (from the Balkans to the Black Sea.) The Galitzianers, in turn, looked down on the Romanians and called them Gypsies from Romania. Hitler did not care where they came from. He burned them all in the same ovens.

We remained Orthodox Jews (from Germany) and many of our friends were Reform Jews, also originally from Germany. In our synagogue women sat behind a partition. We children went inside only to say "hello" to our parents and then played in the fenced-in yard for the rest of the service. Our kitchen was *glatt kosher* (food prepared under strict kosher dietary laws). There was no refrigeration. We had two small food chambers lined with shelves, each one containing a small window, one for meat and one for dairy. It was always cool inside the small chambers.

Before *Rosh Hashanah*, the Jewish New Year, a rabbi would come to the house with a live chicken and wave it over our heads, one

1936 - Bar-Kochba (a Jewish organization)
I am in the second row from bottom,
second child on left seated

1937 – School trip
I am in the center, kneeling

at a time, to cast away our sins. Mother always wore black to synagogue. Papa blessed and kissed each of us before he went to services and Mother cried. On Yom Kippur she also wore the same black silk suit with a handkerchief tied around her wrist. We were not allowed to touch her. During the part of the service where one reads, "It will be decreed, who shall live and who shall die," the wailing and crying from the women's section, coming through the open windows, was terrifying.

Sukkot was a fun holiday in the fall to celebrate the harvest. Uncle Nonny built a *succah* (a booth open to the sky) in the yard of the Schwartzen Adler and we all helped decorate. We all lived in apartments, so during Sukkot we would hang out at Grandma's. All the aunts made goodies and the kids were on their best behavior. Nobody wanted to be barred. Papa brought home a *lulav* (a palm frond), an *esrog* (a yellow citron fruit) in a beautiful box, plus three *hadassim* (myrtle twigs), and two *aravos* (willow branches). We were allowed to hold and shake these items and proudly marched after Papa to synagogue.

On *Simchas Torah* (the holiday marking the completion of the reading of the Torah) we all went to synagogue for treats, but only the boys were allowed to join their fathers in the dancing and singing and in the procession carrying all of the *Torahs* (the Five Books of Moses). We received flags, apples, and candy, much like the current Simchas Torah celebrations in America.

On the first night of *Hanukkah* (the Festival of Lights), we lit the candles and then received *gelt* (coins). Nobody received presents every night for eight days, a later innovation in America. We played a lot with the *dreidel* (a four-sided spinning top) to win hazelnuts and sang all the traditional *Hanukkah* songs in Hebrew.

The cousins came and the cook made lots of potato *latkes* (pancakes) with sour cream.

At *Purim* (a spring holiday), I played Delilah and learned about Queen Esther's victory of good over evil in the Bible. We ate *hamantashen*, a sweet in the shape of evil Haman's three-cornered hat. I seriously considered the stage. We dressed up in costumes and had parties. The grown-ups had a Purim Ball. They dressed in formal attire and danced to German and American dance music and Viennese waltzes. They also raised money for Palestine.

Pesach (holiday of Passover) preparations began weeks before this spring holiday. Dishes were unpacked. Glasses were "koshered" for Passover by soaking them in tubs of water for days. The kitchen was scoured, including the stove. The night before, we burned the *chametz* (the food that is leavened and forbidden on *Pesach*). Little pieces of bread were placed around the apartment. Papa, with us following him, would hold a large wooden spoon and a feather, leading the way with a lit candle, to the little pieces of bread. He brushed the bread into the spoon with the feather, then placed the feather on the spoon and wrapped the whole thing in white cotton and burned it in the stove.

We had large *Seders* (a special ceremonial dinner) on the first two nights of Passover. There were always guests and some Jewish beggars at our table. Papa sat on big pillows and conducted the whole thing except for the "Four Questions." He read the *Haggadah* (small book used for the *Seder*), retelling the story of Moses leading the children of Israel from Egypt, out of slavery. He never skipped a line. I thought it was endless. Naturally we fought over the *afikoman*, the half-piece of *matzah* (unleavened flat cracker) that they hid for the kids to find. We usually ended up sharing the money. We were allowed to drink a little wine; we would fall asleep at the table, only to wake up in time to sing about a little goat.

Mother used to tell a story about one Passover *Seder* at the Schwartzen Adler when her father was still alive. When they opened the door for Elijah, one of their goats walked in. Her brothers had been the culprits and were punished for disrupting the *Seder*.

The holiday of *Shavuos* (anniversary of Moses' receiving the 10 commandments) is celebrated 50 days after Passover. When we finished reading the Torah, we were allowed to take off our wool stockings and put on short socks. It was spring. Gisa and I had new dresses with matching coats. We were allowed to eat ice cream again. Papa had very strict dietary rules: no ice cream in the winter. *Wienies* (hot dogs), salami, and all cold cuts were poison. We only ate them when he was out of town or at friends.

I had my own group of little friends. We had a *kranzchen* (literally a wreath, or better translated as a round circle of our friends). *Fräulein* would serve us hot chocolate and pastries in the world-famous Meissen China cups and we would work on our cross-stitch embroideries. Our parents were all friends. We all went to the German schools and spoke German at home. There were Yiddish speaking girls in the Jewish section of our neighborhood who may not have been fluent in German. But anyway, we identified with Germany and did not speak Yiddish or mix with the Eastern European Jews, the *Ostjuden*. My friends and I were embarrassed by their provincial looks, their clothes, and what we considered odd behavior. How vain and self-important we were. When I was out walking with *Fräulein* one day and stopped to talk to a little girl, *Fräulein* insisted that "those people" were dirty and examined my head for lice.

I was six when my brother was born. Since children were born at home, when my mother went into labor, my father took my sisters and me to Schwartzort. He felt we were too delicate for this event. He took very good care of us. When I stepped on a rake and my foot became infected, he soaked my mother's silk nightgown in 4711 cologne and wrapped it around my foot. When I had a fever, he did the same thing. This time he soaked a washcloth in 4711 cologne and put it on my head. It worked! To this day I think of 4711 as medicinal.

The doctor expected the baby to be stillborn, since my mother was in her mid-forties and he didn't hear the heartbeat. My mother did not believe him, nor would she allow such nonsense. She gave birth to a boy, just as she said. He became her favorite, and could do no wrong. We didn't care. She was so wrapped up in him, we got away with a lot. The event almost closed the town. The crown prince, Misha, always called Butzer in Lithuania, was born. The day of his *bris* (circumcision) my father fed all the town's poor. They were sitting on the wide staircase leading to our apartment. They were sitting on the street. I remember thinking every beggar in the world must be here. My father was very proud. He finally had a son. He ordered a miniature bicycle from England. It had very wide wheels like a motorcycle. Eventually my brother grew into it. It was said that my father walked around with a rail ticket in his pocket, to leave town if mother presented him with another daughter. He lived to regret these words. In later years, he considered his daughters his diamonds and lamented he only had three.

When I was four years old, my father often took me to cafés in the afternoon. (When I was seven and Gisa was four, I was replaced as the apple of my father's eye. I really did not blame him. I was always getting into trouble, and she was very sweet.) His friends fussed over me and filled me with so many sweets that I invariably came home sick. Many times there were entertainers: African-American singers and tap dancers. We did not have any African-American people in our town, so it was very exciting. Some of my father's friends brought their dogs to the café. They sat on chairs at the table just like people and were fussed over like children. This was very acceptable. One friend came with his mistress and that was also acceptable.

One night my parents were entertaining. I was sick with a fever and a sore throat. A scrumptious buffet was prepared, including my favorite pickled herring. I was not allowed to eat herring when I had a fever, another of Papa's dietary laws. I pleaded to be able to just smell it. Nobody believed me when I cried. I had sniffed a peppercorn into my nose. It must have been midnight. Still crying, I was taken to the hospital. The surgeon removed the peppercorn to everyone's shock.

The best of times were the summers in Schwartzort. Children in Europe do not get a two-and-a-half-month vacation. I think we had only six weeks. So when the family moved to the Villa Lieselotte, my sister Fanny and I would commute by boat. We went every weekend.

This little steamer would run up the bay along the Kuhrish Nehrung between the Mainland and Schwartzort, which was about 40 miles above Sandkrug. It was a two-hour ride. It looked like a tugboat and was propelled by a wheel. It took about 30 passengers and a small cargo. It ran on a regular schedule.

The villa sat back off the dirt road in the woods. It had a large iron fence around it. In front were plum trees and the back of the house had a large vegetable garden and an outhouse, since there was no plumbing — no running water. The water pump was outside, too. Cook and *Fräulein* would pump water for the household several times a day, carrying it in buckets. The kitchen was in the basement and each bedroom had washbasins and pitchers. There were also chamber pots for us children, since it was too dark outside to go to the outhouse. We bathed in the ocean. They cooked on a "primus," a small burner fueled with propane gas. There was no oven, therefore no baking. Cakes had to be bought from the mainland. All the berries we gathered in the woods were used to make a lot of jellies and preserves. We had a large brass kettle used only for this. We had no electricity, but it did not get dark until 11 p.m.

Tante (Aunt) Yetta, Papa's aunt, came to stay with us. I think she was supposed to help keep an eye on all the children. She was short and round and wore a long, black dress with lots of petti-

1938 - My two "Kranzchen" friends:
Tamara (left); Debora (right); I am in the center.
Sadly, both friends died in the concentration camps.

coats and a white lace color, even in the summer. She was sweet and we all liked her. She looked as if she came out of a storybook. She had a handsome son, (another) Leo Fleischmann, our cousin. He was very grown up, maybe 20. He had a motorcycle and a gun. He wore a hairnet at night. We thought he was very glamorous. He and *Tante* Yetta lived in Old Town. The young Leo worked for Papa and did not talk much. Papa had brought them from Latvia to live near us and he looked after them. *Tante* Yetta walked with a limp. Her son was very devoted to her.

As soon as we were settled at the villa, Papa left for Karlsbad, Czechoslovakia, for the *kuhr*. As soon as he left, mother started moving in the relatives. She believed all of our cousins to be underprivileged since they lived in the city. They took turns visiting us, one or two at a time. Bathing in the sea was considered very beneficial. It kept you from getting sick in the winter. Mother had a man with a cart bring up barrels of salt water from the sea, which were heated to bathe baby Butzer. We also had large barrels to catch rainwater for washing our hair. It made our hair nice and soft.

Every morning our caravan went to the beach: Mother was first, next *Fräulein*, then all of the children and cousins. It was a major event. They pulled a wagon with towels, clothing, food, and Butzer. It was a half-hour walk, through the forest and over the hill. Most often it was too cold and windy, so we sat behinds the dunes or gathered amber on the beach and jumped the waves. The temperature was usually around 80 degrees in Memel and anything higher was considered a heat wave.

The afternoons were casual. I had time to explore the woods, gather berries, or seek hideouts in the lush foliage of the forest. When my cousins were there, we became more adventurous.

1931- Memel: Party with friends in Memel when Misha ("Butzer")
was born. First man on right is Natan Golden
(my mother's youngest brother) next to Mary Kahn
(my father's older sister, a dentist).

1938 - Memel: Cousin "Bubi" (Manfred) Golden and me "Tutti."
My first boyfriend who stayed in Memel when we fled to America.

He said, "The Modern Romeo and Juliet — unlucky lovers."
"Bubi" did not survive the Holocaust.

We acted out stories. "Hansel and Gretel" was great and so was the story of "The Three Bears." Sometimes we would sneak down to the fishing village.

To the left of the pier was the old fishing village composed of small, weather-beaten houses with tiny yards and small, dirt roads. The local fishermen were old Germans who had lived there for generations. They sold to the summer people and to the mainland. They were not overly friendly and we were told to stay away, but of course, that never stopped us. Old men with leathery, sunbaked, wrinkled faces sat in front of their small cottages mending their nets. Old women stared at us with open hostility and shooed us away.

The rest of the peninsula was a resort, a tourist paradise. There were no cars since Schwartzort could only be reached by boat. Regularly scheduled ships arrived from Memel several times a day. Every evening a large steamship, *The Bremen*, would arrive from Germany. The peninsula was attached to, and had belonged to, Germany until 1923, so Schwartzort remained a popular German vacation spot. I believe it originated in Danzig, now Gdansk, Poland. Every night everyone went to the pier, which was quite large. Both sides of the pier had fruit and sweets stands in the back, like an outside market. They sold locally grown fruit, candy and cakes from the main land, and small smoked fish, caught and smoked in the village. The ships docked in the front of the pier — the event of the day. We would watch the large, white steamship dock. Germans waved while many vacationers disembarked. Porters from various hotels and guesthouses pushed huge hand carts, loaded high with their belongings, to their destinations.

A large, wide dirt road led straight to the *kurhaus* (health resort or spa) in the largest hotel in Schwartzort. The road had many

1992- Beach and dunes still look the same.
Two views of beaches in Memel (Schwartzort),
"Behind the Dunes," protected from the wind

guesthouses and large wooden structures with carved façades. They looked as though they were taken from picture books. The hotel took in vacationers, primarily German. The forest and private homes were tucked away behind the hotel. Many summer rentals were Jews from Memel.

The hotel was a huge, winding wooden structure with verandahs and porches. Outside were tables, chairs, and chaise lounges for informal dining. The formal dining room was also used for afternoon "tea dances" and formal evening dining and dancing.

In the back of the hotel were rows of long, wooden sidewalks lined with doors that had numbers on them. It was a very luxurious hotel, so each room had its own outhouse, with attendants. Everyone was given a key. Around the hotel were small shops — several boutiques and sundries — but the main attraction was the amber found in many stores. Amber was plentiful on the beaches and we would gather it instead of shells. We tested it by rubbing the amber on our clothes and holding it over small bits of paper, like a magnet. If it lifted the paper, it was genuine; if not, we threw it away. The Baltic Sea is world-renown for amber. The shops with amber jewelry attract many tourists.

Nightly, there were dances and entertainment. Many of my parents' friends stayed there. After we had gone to bed, we sneaked out through the back. We watched through the windows as all of those beautiful people danced and had fun. The men did a lot of heel-clicking and hand-kissing, but not their wives' hands, of course.

Some nights, there were excursions to the elk preserve. Horse-drawn, plush-upholstered benches in wagons took us to a part of the Nehrung where large cribs had been erected. They were filled with hay to feed the elk and reindeer. It was a beautiful sight to watch these graceful animals and their young feed by the midnight light at the Baltic Sea, with twilight giving an unearthly feeling to the scene. We encountered the same light on the ship in the North Sea some years later.

Another excursion consisted of a short boat ride to the wandering dunes, high as the pyramids. There were museums and excavations of villages that had been completely buried under the sand of these drifting dunes. There were small houses, their tables set for dinner with plates and cutlery still intact. The people had had to flee for their lives from the sandstorms that covered their village. We loved these trips. We would climb to the top of these sand pyramids and, to my mother's horror, slide down.

Papa returned at the end of the summer, loaded with presents: exotic fruits (peaches wrapped in tissue paper, Jaffa oranges), silk shirts for himself and dresses for Mother from Prague, Czechoslovakia. He brought us beautifully embroidered blouses, also from Czechoslovakia. He never bought by size. If it didn't fit one, often it would fit another. We loved to unpack for him. His friends came out for bridge and Mother would take the boat to Memel to shop for cakes and goodies. This "excursion" would take her the entire day.

In 1936, I was eleven. My sister Fanny was fourteen and very grown up, in my eyes. Papa took her to Brussels, the capital of Belgium, with him. She came back with store-bought clothes and an imitation leopard coat. He also took her to Kovno, the capital of Lithuania at that time. Fanny certainly had a mind of her own. She stamped her foot and got away with whatever she wanted. I think Mother was intimidated by her. Mother was very busy with

Butzer and gave him her undivided attention. Gisa was still the apple of my father's eye, so I was able to pursue my own interests.

The 1936 Olympics were very much in the news. I started to notice that the girls in my class were very blond and athletic. There was much marching and singing of German songs about the *Heimat* or Homeland. I was not invited to many non-Jewish outings, which was not really unusual. We had religion in school – Lutheran. The Jewish children were excused, which made us different. There was a joke to describe someone stupid. Our report cards would say: Religion: outstanding, Attention: adequate. In 1936 a Palestinian Art Show came to Memel. Papa bought a beautiful, large painting of a rabbi. Mother belonged to WIZO, the Women's International Zionist Organization. Fanny belonged to Betar, a Zionist youth group, and she took me along. We wore blue shirts. Uniforms were definitely "in" that year. One morning she made me get up at 5 a.m. Our leader, Jabotinsky, was passing through. We stood shivering on the station platform, our arms outstretched in a salute (much like the Nazis,) but singing a song about *Trumpeldor* (a Zionist activist and war hero).

After the art show, a young woman moved into our home. Many young people from Poland came to Memel to work for a few months, to earn enough money to continue their journey. Memel was a seaport and an exit. The Jewish community would help them find some way to earn the money they needed. She was a *chalutz* (a pioneer) working her way to Palestine. We were to learn to speak Hebrew. She spoke only Hebrew to us and we tormented her. She really earned her money. An English governess came primarily to teach Fanny to speak English. I don't believe she learned much. She was too busy with her boyfriends.

Then *Keren Kayemeth* (Jewish National Fund) boxes appeared in our home. Papa went to England to meet my Aunt Rachel from America. He asked her to sponsor us for immigration, just in case. He felt war was going to engulf Europe. Hitler demanded the return of the province of Memel called Memelland. Lithuania had annexed Memel in 1923. The young Germans kept marching and singing.

I developed a following of about six boys. My two cousins, Peeps and Bubi, were a year older than I. They each wanted to be my boyfriend and had fistfights to see who would walk next to me. There were also Norbert, Izzi, Manfred, and several more; I don't remember their names. They went to the Gymnasium while the girls went to the Lyceum, the German high schools with the highest academic standards. They were private schools with tuition. (Grades K-6 were free.) Upon graduation, one had the equivalent of two years of college. These boys were friends of my cousins, so we were all friends. We started a club. Because I had the best ideas, I was elected president. I was also the only girl. We called it the "The Black Hand." It was a secret organization. We wrote each other letters in invisible ink, played pranks on people, and did harmless mischief. We made stink bombs and left them in the movie house. One Friday I stole the chicken legs from our *Shabbos* (Sabbath) chicken, dipped them into chicken blood, and stamped some writing paper with them. We had a meeting the same afternoon and wrote letters of warning to some people signed, "The Black Hand," under the imprints of the bloody chicken claws and "Tutti Fleischmann, President." We mailed the letters to people at random. We had no stamps, so the post office opened them and called the police.

One afternoon, while mother was at the fish market again and Papa at the bridge club, two men came to our door and showed *Fräulein* their secret police badges. They wanted to talk to Miss Tutti Fleischmann. A trembling *Fräulein* produced me and sent the rest of the household for my parents. The policemen took me into the living room, closed the door, and began to interrogate me. They must have felt pretty ridiculous at the sight of me, a puny eleven-year-old. If they did, they did not let on. They wanted to know the names of the members of my gang, but I stood my ground —I was not talking.

My brother Butzer was hiding on top of the armoire behind the clock, again. Suddenly he piped up, "I know!" and proceeded to name all of my friends. My terrified parents burst into the room. I think the police dropped the case. Nobody else was picked up. The story spread like wildfire through the town. I was labeled a wild tomboy. The girls were not allowed to play with me, including my cousin, Edith, Peep's sister. We were all severely lectured about drawing the attention of the secret police. I was an outcast until soon after, when I became seriously ill and was redeemed.

I came down with diphtheria. Before immunization was available, this was one of the most life-threatening childhood diseases. I was quarantined; the board of health sealed my room. They stuffed cotton all around my door, even the keyhole. Mother and *Fräulein* took turns sitting by my bed. They put on white nurses' coats and covered their hair upon entering my room. At the door was a basin with disinfectant, something to sterilize their hands.

The doctor came every few days to swab everybody's throats for cultures. My culture remained positive for a long time, maybe a month. After a week, my high fever subsided and I started to

Late 1930s, Riga, Latvia: Here is a picture of a family outing
before the war. I am in the driver's seat and Misha
(Butzer) to is to my right, standing.

Photo from 1992 trip back to Lithuania, but woods with ancient
trees have not changed in hundreds of years.

feel better and got bored. I had to remain in quarantine until my culture became negative. Papa ordered a beautiful bicycle for me from England. I spent hours sitting on it in my room, waiting for my culture to become negative. Mother brought me little pillows to embroider. I still have one. I have not been able to look at an embroidery needle since. When I was allowed to join the family again, everyone was so happy to see me. "The Black Hand" was not mentioned again. My brother Butzer and I proudly rode our bicycles up the street and through the forest.

The Germans started to take over. In 1937, Hitler said Memel belonged to Germany and he was going to unite it, or what he called liberation, with the rest of Germany. There was not much the Lithuanian government could do. The whole town was German, even the Jews. My Uncle Nonny, who fought for the Kaiser and earned the Iron Cross, said that they wouldn't bother us and were only after the *Ostjuden*. Everybody seemed to agree, except my Papa.

Papa returned from England after meeting Aunt Rachel from America and announced papers were being prepared for us. In order to obtain permission to immigrate to the United States, an American citizen had to file an affidavit stating that person would be financially responsible for the immigrants. Further documents had to be processed by the American consulate in Lithuania. He explained we would take a long trip to see America until this blew over. Most people agreed that there was nothing to worry about and life went on. I began to notice grown-ups' faces looking serious with a lot of whispering when children were around.

One day mother announced that my cousin Bubi's father, my Uncle Nonny (Levy), was in jail and we were all going to visit him.

We walked over to the jail. There were a lot of people standing on the sidewalk, waving to Uncle Nonny behind the little jail window with bars. His wife, Aunt Frieda, was crying as was Mother and Aunt Resi. I asked my cousin Bubi, "What did your father do?" He told me that his father was caught forging passports and visas for people trying to leave. In Lithuania, exit visas were required with all kinds of taxes attached. Uncle Nonny owned a tavern and knew a lot of people. He was kind and sympathetic. He tried to help some people get out, but was caught forging passports and sent to jail. Our Jewish doctor was also arrested on trumped-up charges of performing illegal operations: abortions.

In 1937, a law was passed forbidding Jews to work in professions. The Lithuania governor vetoed it. Suddenly our German friends turned into Nazis. Clashes between the Lithuanian government, the German population, and the Jews increased. Synagogues were attacked. The Germans slowly started to take over and the Lithuanian government, being outnumbered by the German population, stood by helplessly. Memel was declared a *Frei Stadt*, or free city. That meant the Nazis could demonstrate openly and do as they pleased. Legally we were still under Lithuanian jurisdiction and our property could not be confiscated.

One night, soon after we were told not to go near the windows, a German ship was in port and a demonstration was expected. Papa, who had many friends in high places, had been warned. We did not turn the lights on and sat in the dark. We did not have long to wait. We heard loud singing and marching. Hundreds of boots on the cobblestone streets and hundreds of voices were singing the "Horstwessel," a Nazi song, and the German national anthem.

As they came to our building they raised their fists and shouted, "*Sieg Heil*" (a German salute, literally "Hail, Victory").

We trembled as we peeked behind the closed drapes. They obviously knew Jews lived here. No police appeared, the band of storm troopers was allowed to roam the city, attacking Jews and their property, as they wished. The next morning Fanny and I went to school as usual. The teacher entered the class with the Nazi salute, "Heil Hitler!" The students jumped to their feet with arms raised and returned the salute, "Heil Hitler!" echoed through the school. The Jewish children trembled. Nothing further needed to be said, nor was anything ever explained to us. We just knew that we no longer belonged there. On the way home, I was attacked by several classmates. I was beaten and spit on. They called me "Dirty Jew," but I was not seriously hurt.

Papa was home and we were told we would not be returning to school. Fanny and I would be going to Riga, Latvia, to stay with Papa's sister, Aunt Mary. He would take us soon. Then he would return to Memel to liquidate his assets. He needed to raise as much cash as he could to arrange for our journey. The whole family would join us in Riga and continue to America.

A few days later we went to Kovno, the capital of Lithuania. We all had to appear at the U.S. Consulate in order to receive our immigration papers and visas. There was a problem with Gisa's eyes. We were advised that she needed surgery and might not be permitted to enter the United States. One eye crossed and needed to be corrected. The United States had strict health laws.

Fanny and I went around to say goodbye to everybody. Aunt Henrie cried and said to tell Aunt Rachel to send them papers.

But how could she when Uncle Nonny was in jail? Uncle David, mother's oldest brother, had British passports because my grandfather Moses was a British citizen and so was David. So he, Aunt Rebecca, and their sons, Benn and Siegfried, moved to Dublin, Ireland soon after we left. His daughter, Betty, was married and pregnant and couldn't go with them. Uncle Leo, Aunt Resi, and our four cousins: Morris, Peeps, Edith and Lacka were to move to Rhodesia, South Africa, currently Zimbabwe. Aunt Resi had relatives there and they sent papers that allowed them to emigrate.

They almost waited too long. March 23, 1939, as the Nazis entered the city, they quietly walked out the back door with nothing but the clothes on their backs. They walked all night and finally made their way to Warsaw, Poland and on to South Africa. My grandmother had died the year before, so Uncle Nathan (Natan) was left with Uncle Nonny (Levy) and his family. He was sure nothing was going to happen.

Jews with wealth started to leave Memel. Most went to Kovno; others deeper into Lithuania, taking their money, estimated at 100 million *litas* (Lithuanian currency) with them. In 1938 there had been 6,000 Jews in Memel. When Hitler entered Memel on March 23, 1939, less than half remained. We cried bitterly at the train station. All our friends and relatives came to see us off when Papa took Fanny and me to Riga. It was an overnight trip by train. I was thirteen and I was scared.

IGA

RIGA, THE CAPITAL of Latvia, was a beautiful city.

They called it a miniature Paris. There were wide streets, beautiful shops and cafés, an opera house and a symphony. When we arrived with Papa, we stayed in a big hotel. He had people to see and things to take care of. Fanny was 16 and very pretty. To this day, I don't know how the boys found her. She had dates in the afternoon and at night. I became very sick and had to stay in bed. A female doctor's diagnosis was rheumatic fever. I was running a fever and had swollen knees. Fanny's dates took turns keeping me company. The doctor also said I had a heart murmur. No doctor in the U.S. has ever found the murmur. I was not allowed to write Mother that I was sick. The worst thing was that the hotel had bedbugs. It is an indescribable horror to watch them crawl on the sheet and I became an expert at killing them. I don't know how long I had to stay in bed, but I eventually got well.

Papa went back and forth to Memel to liquidate his business, and we moved into Aunt Mary's, one of Papa's older sisters. She was a dentist, married to uncle Max. They had two children: Gisela, who was my age, and a son, Lazar, who was Fanny's age. He was very shy and scholarly. He barely talked to us. Uncle Max did not speak much either. He was in the jewelry business. I don't think he worked much. He was very sweet.

Also, Papa had two more older sisters, Charlotte and Johanna. Aunt Charlotte, a chemist, was the oldest and widowed. She had two grown daughters. All three wore black and always looked very formidable. She was known to have a sharp tongue and fought with everybody. The family tried to avoid her. We did not see her very much, only when Papa came to Riga. When one of us started a fight, mother would call us Lotte. It meant, "Be careful! You might have inherited this gene."

Aunt Johanna, a pharmacist, was married to Lazar Falkov, who had a jewelry store. They had two children, Sarah and Benn. Sarah was my age and Benn was younger. We did not see very much of them. They lived in a different neighborhood. It was far away and cold. There was always so much snow. We traveled either by tram (streetcar) or we took a *droschke*, a small horse-drawn sled.

Aunt Mary was a lot of fun. We loved her. She had connecting apartments. They lived in one and the other was her dentist's office. My cousin Gisela and I shared a room and Fanny slept with Aunt Mary. Uncle Max slept on the couch for the six months we were there. Aunt Mary and Gisela talked about Fanny's boyfriends all night. Gisela liked classical music. We set our alarm clocks for six a.m. to listen to some broadcast of Toscanini conducting before Gisela went to school. We didn't go because we were refugees and didn't speak Latvian. I don't remember what we did all day — not much. Aunt Mary decided I should become a ballerina and took me to ballet school. We were told that I didn't have the build for the ballet. I was not flat-chested. There went my dream of being a prima ballerina.

The best time was when Gisela and I went to the Christmas Market. It was held outside in the snow and we bought all kind of trinkets and sweets and took a *droschke* home.

Aunt Lena was mother's youngest sister. She also lived in Riga with her violinist husband Volia and her daughter, Marianne, and with his family, a mother and a sister. We privately called her *Aschenputtel* (Cinderella). We visited her several times. She was very sweet. She was always on the floor with a large bucket, washing and scrubbing. Uncle Volia reeked from cologne and wore powder and a hair net. The mother and sister wore long dresses. They sat around in the parlor while poor Aunt Lena worked so hard. Marianne was five years old and still slept in a crib. We thought it was a strange family and felt sorry for Aunt Lena. She always looked like she was going to cry and did so every time she saw Mother.

Fanny was soon the "Belle of Riga." All the Jewish young men were pursuing her. Aunt Mary was her confidant and loved every minute of it. She and her family spoke fluent Latvian, Russian, and German. Nobody spoke Yiddish, nor did we at home, only German. Everyone we met spoke all three languages. No one was afraid of Hitler. Aunt Mary used to say, "We'll open our boarders to Mother Russia. The Russians will protect us, Hitler will never come here." Famous last words.

I was happy when six months later my father came with the rest of the family. We moved into two furnished rooms that we rented from the Jacobsons, another refugee family who rented to us to supplement their meager income. It was very crowded but we were together. Gisa's eye operation was a success and Papa had turned his business over to cousin Leo. They had sold most of our furniture to other Jews who couldn't understand why we were doing this. Mother had bought trousseaus for her three daughters, including the finest china: breakfast, luncheon, and dinner sets in Meissen, Rosenthal, Dresden and Czechoslovakian crystal. Down comforters and paintings were crated and shipped to Indianapolis. So were gifts for Aunt Rachel: silver coffee sets and sable scarves. Everything was heavily taxed by the Lithuanians for export permits and bribes paid for all kinds of permits. Our silver dinnerware ended up in Zimbabwe. We all wore diamonds rings to be sold for cash. We were out of danger!

Papa had been warned by the president of his bank not to go by train through Germany. We would be taken off the train and arrested by the Nazis. So, Papa purchased new tickets and changed our trip. We would go from Riga to Tallinn, Estonia; then to Helsinki, Finland overnight by ship to Stockholm and by train to Oslo, both in Sweden; and finally by ship from Norway to England. We would spend a month in London, then board the Queen Mary in Southampton for New York. He said, "I want you children to remember Europe the way it was. It will never be the same." He was fifty years old, with four children and very little money left after he paid for everything and provided for everybody. He was ready to start a new life in the United States.

Then the unexpected happened. Butzer became ill. He was diagnosed with something wrong with his kidneys; they called it nephritis. They said he couldn't travel; it was "out of the question." They ordered bed rest and the strictest diet. Doctors were called in for consultation and they concurred on no traveling. So the long wait began. We were running out of time. Finally, Butzer was well enough to travel. As we boarded the train to Tallinn, I thought all of Riga came to see us off. Everybody cried and it seemed not just because we were leaving, but out of fear for us, for them, and for the unknown to come. Hitler was rattling the borders of the world. Unspoken fear was in the air and seeping into everyone's very existence.

Our first stop was Tallinn, Estonia, a beautiful small city called Raewald in German. There was a large Jewish community and Papa had many friends who came to see us. Everybody spoke German and made a fuss over us: Herr Fleischmann and his three beautiful daughters. It was *Pesach* and we were invited to a *Seder*. That day Butzer got sick with a fever. Mother stayed in the hotel with him and we went with Papa to the *Seder*. The second night, mother went to the hotel kitchen and got hard-boiled eggs. Somehow, she procured a box of matzah and we had the *Seder* in our room. The next day the doctor said that Butzer could not continue by train or ship, since it was too risky. So a plan was developed. Mother was to fly with Butzer from Tallinn to Sweden. We were to continue to Helsinki, as planned, and we would all meet in Sweden. We all cried when we took them to the airport. Flying in 1939 was, by no means, to be compared with flying today. The "airport" was as big as our backyard. The plane was a little two-engine piper. Mother carried Butzer on and we thought we would never see them again. We were a pretty sad bunch when we boarded the train to Helsinki. Papa's friends tried to cheer us with chocolates when they saw us off, and soon we were able to stuff ourselves with sweets and continue our journey.

Helsinki was very contemporary. Having resisted Russia's communism, it was a thriving seaport with commerce in the western world. So close to the Baltic States, they were always spoken of with one breath and yet so distinctly different. Finnish was the language spoken. We thought of German as being the universal language. Didn't Hitler say, "Tomorrow the world?"

We didn't know what to eat, so we just pointed to the menu and hoped for the best. I still remember the shoes in the store windows. We never saw anything like them: platforms and ankle straps, plus gorgeous dresses and pocketbooks. The next day we boarded a small, luxurious ship for our overnight voyage to Stockholm. The whole interior was in deep blue velvet with highly polished brass fittings, banisters going down steep, spiral staircases. Papa was busy playing cards in the small casino. The three of us had a grand time. Nobody understood us when we spoke in German.

The dining room was mind-boggling. A huge smorgasbord greeted us in the morning. More fish than I knew there were in the sea. Smoked and pickled and cooked, cold smoked meats and cheeses, breads, crackers and rolls that we did not know existed. Papa explained some things were not kosher, but since we were traveling, it was OK. We stuffed ourselves and went on deck to watch the sights. The ship maneuvered through icebergs so close to us that we could almost touch them. It was very scary. I was afraid we would crash into them. It was bitter cold and the light was muted. It was twilight, since the days were still short and the nights very long. It was the end of March. In the Baltic States, darkness comes at 3 p.m. Then, in the summer, the sky doesn't get dark until about 11 p.m. Papa would come on deck and watch with us as the ship glided through the still waters among the glaciers. It was like watching a movie in sepia. He talked to us, mostly saying, "Remember Europe! War is coming and for us a new life, but never forget who we are and where we come from."

We were met and taken to our hotel. Miraculously mother was already there. Both she and Butzer had survived. We traveled in two taxis, one for us and one for our luggage. We had 23 pieces.

Finding each of our own suitcases became a major problem. My travel outfit was a wine-colored suit and a navy sweater. I have not been able to wear those colors again. Papa knew people in all of the countries we passed through. They came to see us at the hotels. He was at home anywhere we went. I came to think of him as "a citizen of the world" — fearless. Nothing seemed to disturb his calm, confident manner. Sweden and Norway passed in a blur. We did not venture far from the hotel because we could not understand the language. Butzer was still confined to his bed and Papa used to give him money to eat his mashed potatoes.

We finally reached England. After docking in Southampton, we took the train to London. Fanny was called upon to translate. My suspicions were correct; she had not learned much. We were met at the station by a man. I presume he was from the travel agency. My father said, "How did you know us?" He replied, "How could I miss you?" We were four kids and had 23 pieces of luggage. We proceeded to the hotel in two taxis; at the hotel we were assigned five rooms. They all looked alike. We slept in a different room every night and never knew whose clothes we would find in the room.

The hotel was on Piccadilly Circle. We had to meet Papa's friends for tea at the hotel on the other side of the circle. Crossing the street seemed an overwhelming task. After a few minutes Papa gave up and hailed a taxi. We drove around the circle to the other side. Tea at the hotel was quite an experience. We had never seen toast, buttered and sliced to finger strips. Sliced, commercial white bread was unknown to us, as was high tea. Our main meal was at one o'clock and a light supper at night. Papa again had many friends in England. He was there twice a year to shop for textiles, especially in Manchester, where most of the textile mills were.

Mother and Butzer remained confined to the hotel but we were taken shopping. We were introduced to the Woolworth store, where we all bought red bathing suits with shirred elastic — They stretched to any size — and raincoats, since it rained every day for the month we were there. Papa introduced us of to his friends and we tried not to look too provincial.

We saw Queen Mary and her two young daughters, Princess Elizabeth and Princess Margaret, in a carriage. For years Mother dressed Gisa and me alike. The dressmaker copied the princesses' clothes from magazines for us. We had several spring outfits just like Elizabeth and Margaret. I remember beige wool dresses with matching coats. Spring is a very long season in the Baltic States. It never gets really hot. We also had the same navy raincoats with silver buttons. Thank heaven the Queen had only two daughters. Fanny never would have dressed like us and Mother would have had a real problem.

After several weeks of much confusion and many mix-ups, we finally took the train to Southampton and boarded the Queen Mary, the most luxurious ship in 1939. Mother and Butzer shared a cabin, we three girls had a cabin, and Papa had his own. It was decided that Butzer remain in bed and stay on a mashed potato diet. He was getting more difficult all the time. Papa continued to pay him to eat and every time we came into his cabin, he would smell our breath to see what we had eaten. We were not familiar with chewing gum, so we all kept a supply of peppermints. Mother remained in the cabin with him during the whole crossing. They had their meals brought in; I guess she too ate only mashed potatoes. With the self-absorption of a fourteen-year-old, I never gave it any thought. The first night, Papa took his three daughters

1939 - Picture of the ship our family took to Norway
instead of going through Germany,
to avoid being arrested by the Nazis.

into the dining room for dinner. We must have looked charming, as everyone smiled at us. The waiters hovered over us and we behaved like ladies. At the end of the meal, small gold bowls with slices of lemons were placed in front of us. We exclaimed, "lemonade!" and drank the finger bowls to the embarrassment of Papa.

The first day out, after breakfast, we were in Mother's cabin, planning our day, when the sirens and bells went off. We opened the door to see what was going on. Fanny was told to use her English to find out what was happening. She didn't understand, but people were running with life jackets. The ship must be sinking!! The steward rushed into our cabin and put life jackets on each of us. Papa appeared and even he looked scared. He tried to communicate with the Steward, to no avail.

Mother cried, "Save yourself and the girls. I will go down with my son." I piped up: "The ship can't sink! Butzer is not allowed to bathe in cold water!" Crying, we were pushed on deck in front of a lifeboat. We held onto one another and Papa kissed us goodbye and recited the *Shema* (a Hebrew prayer declaring one's faith in God). We were all trembling with cold and fear. It was April and the ocean looked rough and formidable. Suddenly the sirens started to wail again. People took off their lifejackets and dispersed. It was only a drill! Laughing, we rushed to tell Mother. It seemed so funny.

The ship was like a huge hotel. There were all kinds of games on deck. I particularly liked horse races and movies. We used to see American movies in Memel, so we knew all the movie stars. I found the swimming pool and went to check it out. I had the beautiful, new red bathing suit bought in England. The pool was the biggest I had ever seen. The water was green. It rolled in the pool with the movement of the ship. I stood there enthralled, watching, when my stomach started to feel queasy. I ran as fast as I could and bumped into the captain on the Grand Staircase where I proceeded to throw up at his feet. The next few days I was seasick. I was also confined to my cabin, too miserable to care. I was told the captain said that it was one of the calmest crossings he remembered.

Then early one morning, Mother came into our cabin to wake us. "Quick, get dressed and come on deck. We are going to pass the Statue of Liberty." The ship passed close to the majestic lady holding her torch. New York appeared in the background. People around us were crying openly, so were my parents. I could not quite understand why, but I knew that this was the most auspicious moment in our lives. We went back to our cabins to dress for our arrival. It took some time to pull into the harbor and dock. Suddenly all was quiet; the engines had stopped. Amidst much commotion we found ourselves in a large room with immigration officials. Mother was still holding Butzer and worried about the doctors: "Will they let him in?" Out of nowhere appeared several important-looking men. My relatives were distributors in the Midwest for the Pepsi-Cola Company, and public relations had come to greet us and help us through the red tape of entering America.

Open Sesame! We walked down the plank into the United States of America. It was April 20th, 1939.* There was Aunt Rachel Domont, a big impressive lady who was my mother's oldest sister. She was with her son, my cousin Ben. He was old, thirty-three, and very handsome. This time it took three taxis and the public relations people to transport us to the Sherry Netherland Hotel, where a suite awaited us to freshen up before we continued our trip by train that evening to Indianapolis, Indiana.

Hitler's 50th birthday.

Pepsi-Cola was bottled by our relatives in Indianapolis for the entire state of Indiana. They owned a large bottling company. They also made their own ginger ale and flavored soda. It seemed they were very rich. Cousin Ben was very good at taking charge, as was Aunt Rachel. He seemed enthralled with his little cousins and spoke a few German words. Aunt Rachel, however, spoke German as well as we did. We did not see much of New York. The buildings were so tall. One could see only a little sky. Looking out the hotel window there was a sea of cars. They looked like a small army of ants crawling along the longest street. That evening we boarded the overnight train to Indianapolis. We shared berths for sleeping and ate in the dining car, served by African-American waiters in white jackets. Again they had the same thin, soft white bread, which I thought was terrific.

The next morning we arrived in Indianapolis, our new home. We were met by our other cousin, Gus, even older at thirty-five, and our Uncle Robert Domont. He was called Boss. He was very grouchy but under his stern demeanor was a heart of gold. He was a real softy and we came to love him. Nobody listened to him or paid much attention to him. They lived in an English Tudor house, very impressive, but too small for all of us. Somehow, we managed to fit in. The first thing Gus did was turn on the record player and taught us the rhumba. He was a great fan of the rhumba.

Ben decided our names needed changing immediately. Fanny became Frances, Sarah was too Jewish, and Tutti was ridiculous. I will never know how he picked the French name, Cherie, for my name. I thought it was an American name until I learned to speak English. He wanted to change Gisela to Gertrude, but she was smart. She wouldn't let him. Misha became Morris.

Later he changed it to Mark. His nickname Butzer disappeared and then reappeared fifty years later on Mark's license plate. He also changed his last name to Fields when he became successful.

Boss came from South Africa to Memel, married Rachel, and had three sons in Memel. They immigrated to America when the children were small. Somehow, they ended up in Indianapolis and opened a small grocery store They also bottled their own ginger ale. Loft Candy Company approached them. They had a syrup they wanted bottled to create a new soda. They were going national and eventually international. Loft planned to enlarge their facilities and give the Domonts a lot of stock in the new company. Aunt Rachel was very smart. "Sure, why not?" The company became the Pepsi-Cola Bottling Company. Even though Boss was illiterate — he could not sign his name and never learned — by 1939 they had a large, modern plant. Both sons were college graduates and ran the business. The Great Depression was on and they accumulated large real estate holdings. Their third son, Julius, had died before we arrived. We never knew him.

INDIANAPOLIS

THE FIRST SUNDAY after our arrival, an open house was held to introduce us. My relatives were prominent members of the Jewish community and the conservative synagogue, Beth El. My Aunt Rachel served on many charitable boards as well as the synagogue's. She and Boss were philanthropic and she had many friends. Many people came to see us. We were the first Europeans they had seen since they immigrated years before. My aunt's friends spoke a mixture of German and Yiddish, so they were understandable. Their children, of course, spoke only English, and we had difficulties communicating.

Among all those people was a young man, Rabbi Elias Charry. He was about 30 years old, very handsome, with a streak of white hair in the center. He spoke perfect German. In the course of the day, he managed to introduce me to several girls my age and arranged for me to join Young Hadassah. Rabbi Charry became our teacher, our friend, and my mentor. He remained thus throughout my life until he died, forty years later.

Aunt Rachel took over our lives. My brother Misha, now Morris, no longer had to stay in bed. Mother ceased to be the center of his universe and she went to luncheons with her sister. The doctor ordered Morris' tonsils removed. He was no longer considered fragile. He had to learn to fend for himself. Papa was considered a "greenhorn" and knew nothing. There was no love lost between him and my aunt; even I could see this.

Morris smashed the Dresden bedroom lamps in a fit of temper, because he was not allowed to go to a luncheon with Aunt Rachel and Mother. It was decided: we had overstayed our welcome. A second-floor apartment in a four-unit building was rented for us. The apartment was tiny and hot. It was 100 degrees in Indianapolis in the summertime and we had never experienced such heat in Lithuania. Gisa and I spent the summer in our red bathing suits sitting in the bathtub while mother brought us Pepsi-Cola. I don't know how the rest of the family managed.

Living in this apartment did not last too long. Aunt Rachel decided that Papa should buy a duplex with his last $10,000. She found one a few blocks from our apartment. The day of settlement, Papa was begging Morris for the money he had given to my brother as bribes to eat his mashed potatoes for about one a year, because of his medical problem with his kidneys. Morris had pockets and boxes stuffed with most of our money. Finally, they made a deal and Papa proceeded to buy the duplex. The upstairs apartment was rented and we settled in downstairs. We had two bedrooms, one bathroom, a breakfast room, dining room, living room, a large porch, and a backyard. My older sister Frances slept in the breakfast room on a sofa bed. My younger sister Gisa and I shared a double bed. Morris, the youngest, slept with Mother in the same room with Papa, who had his own bed in their room.

The furnace was in the basement. It was a coal-burning furnace with heat grates on the floors. The basement was entered through a trap door on the floor of the tiny kitchen. It must have been a closet converted into a kitchen. Mother couldn't even lift the trap door. Papa certainly was not even going to try. He never lifted a finger in his life. They hired an old African-American man who came on winter mornings at 5 a.m. While we slept, he let himself in, went down into the basement, and tended the furnace. He also disposed of the dead mice in the traps. It was a working, middle class neighborhood and we soon made friends. That is, all except Papa. He became a recluse. He was like a fish out of water. The world as he knew it had disappeared. He spent most of his time in bed reading the papers.

Papa was given a job in the Pepsi-Cola plant to check the cases on the truck. Mother made an attempt at housekeeping. She did not have much time. Aunt Rachel took her to all her luncheons with her friends, who fussed over her. Mother was a beautiful woman and very classy. In Indianapolis' Jewish society she stood out, like a rose among dandelions. Her European custom-tailored clothes gave her an elegance that matched her quiet manners.

Rabbi Charry took charge of our education. The summer was over. He accompanied each of us to school, and saw to it that we were put into the right grades. He conferred with the principals. There were no "English as a second language" classes in those days in Indiana. We were placed according to our age. Frances was tested and with a little knowledge of English, had the academic standing of two years of college. She was seventeen and was put into the graduating class. I, at fourteen with even less English, scored the highest grammar grade in my class. It was easy and without exactly knowing what the words meant, I divided the sentence structure as we did in German.

Our life in America had begun. We were making friends. In school we were a novelty. Aunt Rachel's friends included us in their children's parties and activities. We were accepted into a very snobbish Jewish society. They were the Jews who lived on the south side: the Russian and Sephardic Jews. They did not belong to the country club, and we did not date boys from the south side.

I did not have the dresses my friends had. Many times I stayed home from parties at the club because I had nothing to wear. Because Frances was the first to graduate and was of marriageable age, she was excused from everything we had to do or what she did not like. It also meant she had to go to many parties and had to look good, so she needed clothes. Mother somehow managed to buy her a leopard coat. Frances traveled in a well-to-do crowd. I guess they were hoping for an early engagement to a prominent family.

The problem was that it was cold in Indianapolis in the wintertime. Gisa and I also needed coats. Mother had an English wool coat of hers fitted for Gisa. For me, she had a light wool coat fixed up. She had whole mink skins from a scarf put on the collar and down the front. The coat was not really a winter coat, but rather more transitional. I thought it looked gorgeous and pretended it was very warm. I guess I proved that you do not get sick from being half frozen to death. When I stood waiting for a bus, the icy wind blew right through me. To this day, I still feel the cold and love fur coats. My friend's mother kept feeling the coat and asking me if I was warm enough. I lied and told her this was the warmest coat I ever had.

Gisa and I went to Sunday School. I also went to Talmud Torah, a Hebrew school. Children were bussed into the Jewish Community Center for classes. I did not last too long. I had enough with learning English. In no time at all we were speaking English to one another, but at home we still spoke German to Mother and Papa. I cut many classes. I would tell my teacher I did not feel well. I was sent to the office to call home and spoke to mother in German. I would ask something like, "Did I get any mail?" Then I would say to the nurse that mother was home and expecting me. Maybe that was the reason I did not graduate with my class in June, but had to go to summer school for one credit. I graduated in August. I was not the greatest student.

On September 1, 1939, Hitler marched into Poland. We were here in America five months and now we were refugees. Teachers and people asked us questions like, "Did you have ice cream?" or "Did you have bathrooms?" It was incredible how little the people here seemed to know about Europe, especially geography and culture.

Rabbi Charry put me into his Confirmation class. I was able to keep up with my Bible studies and met my friend Jackie. We have remained best friends all our lives. It was a wonderful year for me. At Confirmation, all the girls wore long white gowns; the boys wore dark jackets and white pants. I gave a speech in English and we each had our own table of sweets for the joint reception in the auditorium. At night we had a big party. Aunt Rachel took care of everything. She even borrowed the white gown for me from one of her friends' daughters and they squeezed me into it. She invited all her friends and they gave me gifts. Aunt Rachel was very happy. She had been giving gifts to her friends' children for years and felt they owed her because she had no daughters. She was looking forward to the three of us becoming engaged, so she could make showers.

I babysat for fifty cents a night, sometimes until one or two in the morning. I saved my money. Every *Rosh Hashanah* my friends got new clothes for the fall and I bought a new dress with my baby-sitting money. I also bought a hat, because Rabbi Charry made us wear hats to services.

Everybody went to services on Friday nights, including my cousins. The Jewish community was closely knit, except for the Jews from the south side. Again the Jewish snobbery reared its ugly head. I was not allowed to date anyone who was not cleared by my aunt. So they lived separately, just like in Memel. There were no Sephardic Jews in the only Jewish country club. (I am happy to say all this has changed since we lived there.) I received an invitation to a party from a very nice boy. He lived in a beautiful, big house on a beautiful street. I was the envy of all my friends, since they were not invited. I was very excited and asked permission to attend. Mother checked with my aunt. Permission denied. The boys' grandmother had been our butter-and-egg woman in Memel. I suppose, my aunt and uncle held onto their past lives without rhyme or reason. Their former status in Europe comforted them. By contrast, in Indianapolis we were financially depleted, having spent all our money just to get to the United States.

But we were all having a great time; I gave little thought to my parents. Then, Papa fell off the large Pepsi-Cola truck one day while he was counting the cases. He broke his leg in several places. He remained in bed for months. He barely spoke to us. My friends were afraid of him. He never spoke to them. He was in a deep depression. We lived on $11 a week of insurance money for a family of six.

Every Friday, Boss would be driven up in a Pepsi-Cola pickup truck. The driver would bring in a case of Pepsi-Cola, a chicken, and a *challah* (braided bread for the Sabbath). The rest of the week we ate ground meat or macaroni and cheese. Sometimes mother would cook gefilte fish. Gisa and I would fight to deliver it to Boss. He always gave us a $5 bill and mumbled something like, "You need new shoes." After school, my friends and I went to their homes to listen to music and their mothers served snacks. I never asked them to our house, since we didn't have any snacks or extra food. Once Papa brought home a box of cookies. They were called Cat Tongues, the same name as a very fine German chocolate. They turned out to be dog biscuits. Fortunately, Frances' girlfriend was there to explain and no harm was done.

The diamond rings from Memel that we wore to sell were not saleable in America. There were newer cuts here to enhance the stones and make them appear larger. All our fine china and crystal arrived shattered. We were insured, but public relations arranged to have customs waived for us, so the crates were not opened. The insurance company claimed everything was broken by the railroad from New York to Indianapolis, not by the ship. So we were paid ten cents per pound. It came to about $300. My parents were too devastated to do anything and our relatives too disinterested.

My father withdrew from the world more and more. Only Gisa clung to him and comforted him, as well as a twelve-year-old could. Mother was also trying to cope. She had to learn to cook.

Picture of my sister Fanny's passport to gain entry into the United States

In America our name became Fleischman, with only one "n." Cousin Ben changed Fanny to Frances, Gisela kept her name, and Butzer (nee Misha) became Morris. My name Sarah (Tutti) became Cherie. I did not need a passport, because I was young enough to be listed on my father's passport.

Photo of me, now called Cherie, in high school
(about 1940)

She did not know how to clean, so nothing was cleaned. She sent all our clothes to the laundry and our custom-made wool dresses came back shrunk to a doll's size. Aunt Rachel expected her to be at her beck and call. That put a strain on my parents' marriage. She and her husband, Boss, took mother alone to Florida for the winter. We fended for ourselves as best we could. At first, we were boarded out for dinner. Morris started throwing up and Papa didn't go; Gisa became the cook. She shaped chopped meat to look like a chicken. Since Boss was in Florida for the winter, there were no chicken and Pepsi deliveries on Fridays.

Somehow, we survived the winter. We were pretty much on our own. Frances and I had our own crowds. We went to parties and rode around in cars. My girlfriend was 15 and did not have a license, but she drove us anyway. We went on hayrides and to dances. We developed hay fever.

We thought Indianapolis was heaven. We were free, living in the United States, without almost any parental supervision. Gisa took care of Morris. She was big for her age and miserable. Our clothes did not fit her. She was taller than us. She took to sewing peasant skirts. My parents were so engulfed in their own misery, they simply could not cope with us. Morris started his own business with the help of his best friend David. They kidnapped dogs and returned them for "rewards." Many nights, Frances and I tried to sneak back in the house much later then we were supposed to be in our beds. We crept into the bathroom in the dark only to be attacked by a dog.

December 7, 1941, we were sitting around the dining room table. My boyfriend came in and told us the Japanese had attacked Pearl Harbor. I had no idea where it was and what it meant. Papa knew.

He said we were in it now and the U.S. would finish Hitler. He seemed to perk up after that and always had his head in the paper. He seemed to read English and understand it. He even had the truck drivers from the plant over for poker one night when mother was in Florida. The three of us had to clean up the next morning. We tied scarves over our noses. The smell of cigars and beer made us sick. I think he thought, "We will be going back soon."

On Saturdays my girlfriends and I would get up early. We packed sandwiches (on white bread with mayonnaise) and took the bus downtown to the movies. The Lyric had a movie and a stage show with the big bands. We would get there early so we could get seats in the front and stay for two stage shows. After the show, we would go backstage for autographs.

One Saturday, we went to see Tommy Dorsey. After the show, as usual, we went backstage. Everybody was crowding around Buddy Rich, the drummer, and the Pied Pipers, the singers. I saw this skinny young kid standing by himself to the side. Nobody was paying any attention to him. He looked about my age. I felt sorry for him and went over and asked him for his autograph. He was happy to oblige. He wrote, "To Cherie, Sincerely Yours, Frank Sinatra." At the time, I considered it my *mitzvah* (good deed) for the day. Much later, when Frank Sinatra appeared at the Paramount in New York, I think Morris sold my autograph of Sinatra.

The discord between Mama and Papa widened. Mother continued to be at Aunt Rachel's beck and call. Boss had a circulatory disease and his legs were amputated. Aunt Rachel asked Mother frequently to go to Florida to keep him company. My mother was not able to refuse her and we were left to cope as well as we could, again. Papa's depression worsened and he seemed to be unable to function any further. When Gisa came home from school one day, she found him on the sofa in the breakfast room with all the gas jets opened. A letter to Aunt Mary was on the table. He recovered, but a few days later, he disappeared. Gisa was thirteen. Mother sent her downtown to look for him in all the rooming houses. They looked in the parks and bars. They combed the city for him. I was very upset because I had to stay home with Morris. I had a heavy date. My boyfriend was being installed as president of AZA, a Jewish fraternity, and there was a dinner dance. I had to break my date. They found Papa late that night; I don't know what transpired. Papa left for New York. He was going to establish himself and we were to follow. Gisa did not stop crying and fighting with Mother, so soon after, she, too, moved to New York to be with him. I continued to block all unpleasantness.

In New York, they rented a room with a refugee family. Papa sent Gisa to school in a cab every day. He started a manufacturing business. World War II was on. The soldiers needed a small bag — hand luggage — so the furlough bag came to be. He found a pattern maker and a cutter who did this at night for him. He found many refugee women who spoke no English and needed an income. They sewed the bags at home. He went around dispensing materials and picking up finished products. He also saw buyers and took orders. Soon he found himself a partner and they rented a loft off Fifth Ave. on 8th St. They called themselves the F & F Bag Co., for Fleischman and Finkelstein, his new partner, and they hired a salesman, who opened large accounts in stores like Woolworth and other chain stores. They expanded to making wallets and cosmetic bags. Six months later, Papa sent for us. A beautifully furnished, 10-room apartment was waiting for us. The Upper West Side was an elegant neighborhood in 1943. Our apartment had maid quarters, where Morris was installed, and large, airy rooms. Papa had completely furnished the whole place himself, including some fine antique pieces. The lobby was marble with thick red carpets, three elevators with operators, and a doorman.

I did not move with everybody. I had three months until graduation. (I guess I cut too many classes and had to go to summer school.) I overheard my parents say, "Cherie will never pass the New York Regents." I was left with Aunt Rachel. Finally, after I graduated, I joined them feeling not on par intellectually with the rest of the family. I was told not to get a job, but first to get to know the city and learn the subway system. I took the wrong train and found myself in Harlem in the middle of a race riot. I guess I flunked. I got paid to drink my orange juice. Gisa was working, so I could borrow money for lunch at the Stork Club. Frances did not work either. We had a great time exploring New York. We had ice cream in Schrafft's, Rumpelmayer's, and all the best places. We walked 5th Avenue in the Easter Parade, saw the now popular Frank Sinatra at the Paramount, and finally found jobs and went to work every day.

Papa was his old self again. He knew the best restaurants in New York. The Russian Tearoom was his favorite. People were always dropping in. He had many friends again. Boys from Indianapolis going overseas came to us. Girlfriends who had boyfriends going overseas came to stay with us. Papa loved them all. "Call me Leo," he would tell them. He was charming and they loved him. On any Sunday morning you could find card games going on. The big table in the dining room always had a dozen people around it. The solders played poker, but Papa loved bridge. He returned to playing at the bridge clubs. He was a fabulous player and always in demand and always winning.

Life for us was good again. Many Europeans lived in New York. Mother's friends spoke mostly German and came to tea with their boxes of Barton's chocolates. Papa loved America. He loved Roosevelt. He was a Democrat. He never failed to vote. He praised his new country but kept warning: "Do not trust Russia! They will turn against us, and when the war is over, they will keep us armed and dangerous."

I married first. My husband, Joe, went overseas one week later. I remained at home. Soon after, Frances married Sy. They had a beautiful apartment on Riverside Drive, near us. Finally the war was over and Gisa married her Joe.

Stories of the Holocaust started to reach us. We received a letter from Aunt Johanna, one of Papa's older sisters. Their family was saved. They had fled into Siberia and then came to America — nothing from the others. They were presumed dead. The newspapers were filled with stories and pictures of liberated camps and atrocities performed by the Germans and Lithuanians and Latvians. Old friends from Memel came to see us. They had survived. They told stories. Uncle Nathan was shot trying to escape the Kovno Ghetto. Cousin Leo was seen being "relocated." It was later documented that he was trying to escape from a camp in Riga, recaptured by guards with dogs, shot, and hanged. Papa contacted HIAS (the Hebrew Immigrant Aid Society) for survivor lists. He found friends in Shanghai and sent them papers. From our families there was nothing; they were gone. My parents sat *shivah* (the mourning period for the dead).

For almost 50 years we never spoke of Memel: not among ourselves, not to our children. We never spoke of our childhood. We were survivors, but did not even admit it to ourselves. The silent guilt of the survivors was upon us. How did Papa know we must leave? Could he have foreseen such horror? I look at the pictures of the camps and say, "There but by the grace of God were we." I have said the *Kaddish* (an ancient prayer recited by Jewish mourners) at Yad Vashem in Israel, at the U.S. Holocaust Memorial Museum in Washington, D.C., and at the graves of my grandparents in a restored cemetery in Memel. At *Yizkor* memorial services, I see them all and say their names: Uncle Nonny, Aunt Frieda, cousin Bubi, Hennie, Tante Yetta, cousin Leo, Betty, Uncle Nathan, Aunt Lena, Marianne, Aunt Mary, Gisela, Max, Lazar, Aunt Charlotte and her daughters. I see my friends' faces. I have forgotten many names.

Many questions remain unanswered: Could Aunt Rachel have saved more? The world stood by and did nothing. Where was American Jewry? Nobody was marching on Washington. The fact remains that the Nazis could not have killed all the Jews without the help of the Lithuanians, the Latvians, the Estonians, and the world. The Holocaust is being taught in our schools. Is this collective guilt??

EPILOGUE

FRANCES AND I went back to Memel and Riga in 1992. We walked both cities by memory. There had been heavy fighting in Memel during WWII. Much was bombed. The Schwartzen Adler is gone. A large market place is still there, the Friedrichmark. The old part is restored as Altstadt, painted in pastels, as a modern architect thought it should have looked. We found the Jewish cemetery. It was destroyed, all the tombstones had been ground up. They said the Russians did it. The Lithuanians found six remaining graves. They erected a monument. Our grandparents' stone was one of them. As Thomas Wolfe said, "You can't go home again."

The Baltic Sea is still beautiful, but polluted. We found an old lady, a survivor in Riga. She was a relative of Falcove, my father's family name. She told us Cousin Beno lives in Israel. Cousin Gisela is still in Latvia. She did not know where or her married name. She was living on $20 a month in a bare room. The war had not ended for her. There is no compensation money for her, although the German veterans receive a pension.

My mother became Nanny, a legend of her own. She lived to be 104 years, beloved by all. Papa became Papi Leo. He died at 72, still a young man. We all mourned his sudden death for a long time. This, my dear children, is your heritage. I will say to you what my father said to us crossing from Finland to Sweden: "Remember!!"

Returning to Memel reminded me that the life we enjoyed as children was truly "a time to keep" in our memories.

Photos taken in 1992, when my older sister Frances (bottom) and I (top) went back to Lithuania for the first time since our family's flight in 1939. Places had not changed, except for places that had been bombed.

1992 - The Baltic Sea looks the same, but now is polluted.

1992 - Harbor of Memel — no change

Going back to Schwartzort
1992- The Bay along the "Kuhrische Narung"

1992 - Pier in Schwartzort (top) — no change

1992 - House in fishing village near Schwartzort

1992- Street in Riga: Latvia still looks the same as in the 1930s.

1992- Jewish school my mother, Judith Golden, attended in 1895
in Memel. Still standing!

1992- Cemetery plaque in Memel's Jewish cemetery,
restored by Lithuania.
Taken when Frances and I returned to Lithuania
for the first time since 1939.

Cherie Goren

ACKNOWLEDGMENTS

THE REPUBLISHING of this book would have been impossible without the Go Fund Me! and personal donations by the following:

Anonymous (friend), Eileen Akin, Flora Cowen, Lyndon Cramer, Joyce Eisenberg, Daniel Falcone, Susan Freimark, Carolyn Friedman, Teresa Funke, Suza Francina, Diane & Larry Gall, Jerome Henkin, Alan Jacobson, Carol Knopf, Jeffrey Knopf & Christina Milburn, Dr. Harry Knopf, Bob & Friedhilde Milburn, Anne Lawrence, Susan Lieberman, Renee Locks, Sylvia McKinnon, Suzanne McQueen, Bernice Moss, Anna O'Brien, Debra O'Conner, Max & Joel Orland, Maura Roessner & Basha Starr, Risa Rohrberger, Irma Shapiro, Prof. Arthur Shostak, Ira & Samantha Spivack, Dr. Sheldon & Joan Kaplan, Rosie & Barry Wiener, Emily Zurlnick, and (Maestro) Zeitlin's Recorder Class.

Any donations received after our first printing will be added in a later printing.

LINKS
SPECIAL NOTES

In 2018, Fred Finkelstein, Cherie's nephew, produced and directed a documentary film about Cherie's life in Memel, Lithuania. *Leaving Memel: Refugees from the Reich* traces the story of the Golden-Fleischmann families in Lithuania and captures their abrupt departure from Europe on the eve of Hitler's rise to power. It will soon be available as a DVD/Blu-Ray disc. For more information please contact Fred at: ff@sparklestone.org or visit his web site: www.sparklestone.org

Granddaughter Leah Goren created an artistic rendition of this photo in her article about her grandmother that appeared in the *New York Times* in 2018. Link to the article and art work: https://www.nytimes.com/2018/11/05/opinion/i-want-you-to-remember.html.

Son-in-law Max Heffler has several sites with more information on Cherie's family tree. This one Max sent is Moses & Kende Isikowitz Golden in the geni One World Family Tree and has photos:

https://www.geni.com/family-tree/index/5299517694440020886

Here I am with my editor Ellen Sue (on the right),
after a good session of collaboration and editing.
Krista, my book designer, captured the moment with this photo.

46161974R00057

Made in the USA
Middletown, DE
26 May 2019